LONE STAR CHRISTMAS:
SEASONAL EDITORIALS
of
FRANK GRIMES

Edited by
CHARLES H. MARLER

Foreword by
A.C. GREENE

Illustrated by
RUTH JACKSON

Typesetting, *Mel Ristau/Design*
Illustrations, *Ruth Jackson*
Printed in the United States of America

Grimes, Frank, 1891-1961.
    Lone Star Christmas: Seasonal editorials of Frank Grimes / edited by Charles H. Marler; foreword by A.C. Greene.
        p. cm.
    ISBN 0-89112-092-0
        1. Texas--Social life and customs. 2. Christmas -- Texas.
I. Marler, Charles H. (Charles Herbert) II. Title.
F391.G85 1989
394.2'68282'09764--dc20   89-38696
                                                 CIP

To the Grimes sons and daughters
Capt. Rudyard Kipling Grimes
Dr. Mary Xantha Grimes
Frances Grimes Topel
Lt. Gen. Wm. Oscar Senter

CONTENTS

FRANK GRIMES, EDITORIALIST

Even as a boy, I wanted to become a reporter. In Abilene, my family lived across the street from two sisters who were about my mother's age and were her friends. These sisters had a dashing brother, Charlie, who drove a red convertible and was a sports writer. One day, when I was about six years old, Charlie took me with him to visit football workouts around town. I'm not sure whether it was the red convertible or the confident way he approached coaches and players—but something convinced me I wanted to follow in the scribe's footsteps.

Later, I engaged in that quasi-journalistic activity of so many American youngsters . . . I delivered the daily papers. How many times did I laboriously pump my balloon-tired Schwinn from one corner of town to the other. I still have good legs from that labor. But I gained something more important than strong legs: I became a newspaper reader. Ironically enough, it was an opinionated columnist in a non-Abilene paper that caused me to begin reading the editorial pages—and to discover Frank Grimes.

That opinionated non-Abilene columnist enraged me with his unfair (in my eyes) attacks on everything from Social Security to Franklin D. Roosevelt, and when, almost by chance, I read the Abilene newspaper's editorial pages, I realized that whoever was writing the Abilene editorials outstripped the big city editorialist. He was not only a smoother craftsman with genius writing ability and artistic humanity: even a smart-aleck teenager perceived Frank Grimes to be wise. And I never had to change my mind.

My own newspaper career was not meteoric in its rising. I did my first work on the college paper and in World War II, I edited a small Navy publication more because I could type than because of skill. I finished Abilene Christian College in 1948 and was heading for Salida, Colorado, to take a high school teaching job ... when I became worried about the braking capability of my car, a yellow Rolls Royce convertible. I stopped in Abilene en route from Dallas, by then my home, and discovered the mechanic couldn't take the wheels off a Rolls in less than six weeks, so I had to tide myself over waiting for my car to be looked at. I got a job bottling Coca Cola, and one noon in downtown Abilene, after confronting a fellow graduate who was obviously prospering at something well above my speed, I marched upstairs to the *Reporter-News* city room, applied for a job, and talked my way aboard at $35 per week. Two of the greatest events of my life followed within ten days of that employment: I renewed acquaintance with a fetchingly darling girl named Betty I had met at a Hardin-Simmons University night class the year before—who was to be my wife for thirty-nine years—and I finally met Frank Grimes.

Although he kept very much to himself in his office, the only private office in the city room, I dared introduce myself, telling him I was a native of Abilene (the only native on the staff, at that time) and had been reading him since high school. History was the first topic we explored, then gradually our conversations edged onto comparative politics, the potential treachery of the newspaper business (he despised the word "journalism"), and eventually we grazed over many green pastures of philosophy, life and the human comedy.

It was hard for a young person to get to know Frank Grimes, not because he disliked the young but because his comments were so cogent and centerpointed a young hotspur couldn't find weapons to duel him with, in case the hotspur liked to argue—as what hotspur doesn't? Fortunately, I was assisted by the occasional presence of the fetching darling from H-SU, who found it easier to approach Frank Grimes than I did. By the spring of 1950, when darling Betty and I were married, Frank Grimes had assumed a place in both our lives that transcended our careers. I say, not boasting (although it is something to boast of), he grew to be more than my

mentor; ours was that rare instance of an older profes-
sional who takes a younger one as friend ... as friend
almost of a standing with that roundtable of cronies he'd
known and gamed with for decades at the old Abilene
Club. His wedding gift to Betty was a Better Homes &
Gardens cookbook, which, he explained to her, would
help her tame a young husband, who despite infatuation
(he sagely suggested) might take a bit o' taming.

I never wrote an editorial during those Abilene
years, but he cast my die, so to speak. After Frank
Grimes, I knew that if I continued in the news business,
it would be as an editorialist. He was a realist, but not a
cynic, and I learned to divert my own strong inclinations
in that goalless direction. His realism was human, ac-
cepting the weaknesses but acknowledging the strengths
of human life. His language could be strong, and he
could exhibit outrage, but he knew that no matter how
terrible or how wonderful the news was, day by day, year
by year, it was always a human story, something happen-
ing not to gods or devils, but to people ... the same sort
of people who might live in Africa, Europe, Asia ... or
Abilene, Texas. This did not make him a gentle philoso-
pher, but it made him understanding. He rejoiced in life,
and looked back in love, not anger, even when anger
might have been earned. His own life had taught him
many bitter lessons, and while he never referred to them

4

in his writings, they toned and diluted the acid that could have corroded his views. He accepted the idiosyncrasies of the men and women who were his readers and the humorous fragility of the editorialist's role. In my favorite of his writings, he laments that during his millions of words in print, he had launched many a missle and waited, half-fearfully, for it to explode, only (in his words) to have it "fall in quiet pools of public inattention." But let an editorialist abjure pumpkin pie (as he had done), and the wrath descending on his head could be fearful to observe.

Frank Grimes never won a Pulitzer Prize, or any of the other national awards that are mostly parceled out on a calculated basis. And one of my greatest personal disappointments was that he did not live to caution and cajole me when I took over the editorial pages of the *Dallas Times Herald* and later functioned as editorial commentator on radio and television. It was not a matter of pride, it was only a lament for the loss of his guidance. After all, my being there at all was mainly his doing.

A.C. GREENE

A Typewriter Santa Claus

Christmas seasons from the 1890s through 1960, the lifespan of Frank Grimes, helped the Abilene editor and poet to generate more than 200 holiday editorials on his typewriter. Readers will find his seasonal editorials a rich source of the spirit and memories of country and small-town Christmases celebrated by Texans between the Antebellum experience of his parents and the Space Age.

Grimes' Christmas editorials reveal the heart of several aspects of this "morning of mornings" in American life; he deals with the spiritual, economic, cultural, psychological and technological facets of our way of life as revealed in our customs of giving and receiving. The principal themes of his Christmas editorials are the gift of Christ Jesus, the spirit of generosity, the magical role of Christmas in the lives of children, and seasonal safety.

The Grimes editorials in the *Abilene Reporter-News* from 1923-60 trace, through the Christmas experience, the impact upon the people of the nation's economy, of worldwide military conflict, and of the development of technology and products, which by the end of Grimes' life had revolutionized the Christmas he had known as a boy. To read this collection is a rich sociological tour.

He regreted, not only the disappearance of the joy caused by an orange in a Christmas stocking, but the increasing commercialization of the holiday. However, he was realistic enough to admit that Christmas could not be turned back to simpler times; he knew holidays reflected the times and the culture. His nostalgia, nevertheless, caused him once to quote the poet Elizabeth Akers Allen, "Backward, turn backward O Time, in thy flight; make me a child again, just for tonight!"

Nostalgia, Grimes wrote, is a central part of the Christmas celebration for adults because they see the Christmases of their childhood as unique reference points in their lives. The editorials of his last decade of writing, particularly, are rich in the nostalgic element because in the 1950s he perfected the emotional appeal in his editorials. His most recognized Christmas editorial was a 1955 piece titled "Christmas at Copperas Cove," a masterpiece of wistfulness and O. Henry-style storytelling, which was honored by the Texas Associated Press as the outstanding editorial in the state that year.

Grimes' personal experiences were rooted in the Southern background of his father and mother. His father, who at age 16 was a scout for General Nathan Bedford Forrest in the Civil War, was a Methodist circuit rider. Frank was the fifth of 12 children of the preacher. The boyhood Christmases of Frank, necessarily, imprinted upon the editor the spiritual element of the season, an appreciation for small acts of generosity, and a love of the scents of Christmas.

The Abilene editor spent most of his early Christmases in Central Texas, but in 1914 he moved permanently to Abilene in West Texas. He was father and Santa Claus to one stepson, a son and two daughters: General Wm. Oscar Senter; Captain Rudyard Kipling Grimes, who died in a Japanese prison camp after the fall of Corregidor; and Mary Xantha and Frances.

He edited the *Reporter-News* in 1920-61. A finalist in the Pulitzer Prize editorial contest of 1951, he also published poetry, and his most noted work today is a piece of folk-meteorology titled "The Old Mesquites Ain't Out," which the *Abilene Reporter-News* still publishes every spring.

He lost the 1951 Pulitzer editorial writing contest because Arthur Krock of the *New York Times* did not believe a Southwesterner could write six superior quality editorials every day. Grimes rejoined philosophically in an editorial titled "Often a Bridesmaid, Never a Bride."

Texans enjoyed the last Frank Grimes Christmas essay December 23, 1960, written in his tuberculosis sanatorium room in San Angelo—a Yuletide gift from their typewriter Santa Claus.

CHARLES H. MARLER

10

A WHILE BACK

December 21, 1923

How many Christmas presents are you giving this year? Last night Friend Wife showed us the complete list of presents that are being given by all members of our family. When it was handed to us, we thought at first it was an inventory of our household furnishings.

Our mind slipped back to the simplicity of some of the oldtime Christmases.

In particular we recalled the finest Christmas we ever had. We were a boy then. Most of the presents were home-made. Grandma furnished mittens, knitted by oil lamp after we'd been tucked in bed—thick warm mittens with a long cord that extended up through coat sleeves and around the neck to prevent loss. Aunt Saphronia gave us a basket of Christmas cookies, shaped like animals and stars and covered with delicious colored sugar.

Uncle Tom gave us a watch, and his generosity appalled us even if it was the old turnip that he'd discarded. You can imagine the reaction you'd get if you tried giving a 1923 boy a second-hand timepiece.

Most of the presents were useful, in the old days, including a reefer raincoat and a new pair of shoes. As for "boughten" presents, they were limited to "The Erie Train Boy" by Alger, Henty's "With Clive in India," a New Testament and that most wonderful of old-time toys, a tin monkey that climbed a string.

At that, Christmas of long ago represented proportionately as big an outlay as now, comparing the family incomes of the two periods.

But the gift itself was secondary to the spirit of the giver, far more than in the present generation. Somehow, we believe the Christmas dinners of those days were superior. The Christmas eve entertainment at the church was as enjoyable, to us, as the modern movie.

Christmas has changed, but no more so than the rest of life. An advancing standard of living has its price.

CHRISTMAS HASN'T CHANGED

December 24, 1925

"It doesn't seem like Christmas any more," wails the fat man, well on toward fifty. "I just can't get into the spirit of the thing anymore; it doesn't seem like it used to when I was a kid."

Of course not. We are kids no longer. We lack the trusting outlook on life that we had when we were kids. Christmas no longer seems like Christmas to us, not because Christmas has changed but because we have changed.

As a child, a few sticks of peppermint candy, a rag doll or a tinny contraption that was meant to resemble red horses attached immovably to a blue fire wagon, a few Roman candles (only we called them "cannons") and a package or two of firecrackers made up a complete Christmas for us. We got more of the joy of possession out of them than we could get out of automobiles and diamond rings and houses and lots, now that we're grown up. And "a nairgun" or a pair of red-topped boots brought a bigger thrill to our little breasts than John D. Rockefeller gets out of endowing a new University.

13

You remember the old time Christmas. Somehow
during the night before, as you slept three-abed with
your elder and younger brothers, Santa Claus made a
mysterious entrance through the fireplace and loaded up
your stockings with candy and nuts and suchlike. Bright
and early on the morning of mornings, some heroic
volunteer (probably Dad) rolled out of bed bright and
early and built a roaring fire in the old fireplace. Then
you bounced out of bed and took possession of your
kingdom—the kingdom of toys and trinkets; of make-
believe. Breakfast was forgotten.

Along about nine o'clock Aunt Emma arrived with her numerous progeny, each loaded down with things Santa Claus had brought them. Then until dinnertime the children would display their presents, perhaps quarrel over them a bit. At high noon came the Christmas dinner, with its turkey and dressing and frills and furbelows.

Christmas night there'd be a big pyrotechnic display, perhaps a Roman candle fight between rival grown-up groups, with much scorching of overcoats and mittens.

Verily, Christmas "ain't what she used to be," but Christmas itself isn't to blame. Our scientists should develop some system of keeping us from growing up.

CHILDHOOD'S HOLY WRAITH

December 13, 1926

We sprint here and there through crowded, gasping stores, we thrust loiterers with our elbow, we push venerable ladies away from handkerchief counters, we hurl imprecations at traffic jams, and we feverishly label Christmas the biggest commercial plot of the ages.

But—and this "but" is everlasting—

A tiny wraith persistently pursues us, a rollicking, carefree wraith that we cannot shake off. It hovers just over the rocking horses, the electric trains, the drums and the horns in the department stores.

It shines back at us out of the faces of the boys and girls we see on the streets or at play indoors on these long winter evenings.

Its ghost leaps out of the past to allure us to tinker with a mechanical steam shovel or a "mama" doll that we come across as we hunt gifts for "Aunt Emma's boy and girl, William and Mary."

It is a wraith that we never can elude, no matter how old or how cross we are. Its clean, fresh face laughs at our frowns.

When we sit by the fireside watching the bewitching figures that leap and dance in the crackling flames, the wraith mocks us. Or pleasantly, it takes our hands and wends along the old, familiar street whereon we knew every house and every tree and every single face that passes.

It is the wraith of our childhood, and we never can quite escape its charm.

SANTA CLAUS

December 15, 1926

How did this Santa Claus business originate, anyway? We all know there is a Santa Claus, but few know how he got started out in the business of making children and grown-ups happy along about Christmas time.

Santa Claus is a Dutch corruption of Saint Nicholas, the history books tell us. Saint Nicholas was a Roman Catholic bishop who died early in the fourth century, A.D. He is supposed to have been a bishop in a small corner of Asia Minor. Traditions of his miraculous powers were widespread throughout the East and the West, and his feast day was set on December 6. As this date was near to Christmas, and as Saint Nicholas had a reputation of being a generous, charitable being who went about dispensing gifts and good cheer to all and sundry, it wasn't long until his name and fame were associated with Christmas, and he became the patron saint of childhood, the bearer of gifts to the children on Christmas.

Saint Nicholas is the patron saint of the Russian church, of scholars, clerks, travelers, sailors and pawn-brokers.

As Santa Claus, the good Saint Nicholas typifies the spirit of Christmas—the one time in the year when every human being, no matter how poor and hopeless, catches a glimpse of that brighter, farther shore where the ills of earth shall be righted and trouble and terror and tribulation shall vex us no more. Saint Nicholas, Kris Kringle or Santa Claus, they are all the same, and the world is better for the spirit that evokes their presence.

THE ETERNAL EMPIRE

December 25, 1927

Every person should read General Lew Wallace's "Ben Hur" in order to gain a just and simple explanation of the significance of the day we celebrate on December 25 each year.

In the midst of pre-Christmas and post-Christmas activities we are apt to forget or disregard the true meaning of this great holiday.

Christmas has become a time of feasting and jollification, instead of a time of fasting and prayer.

It should be a time of rejoicing, to be sure, but not a time of riotous celebration.

We have commercialized Christmas.

The giving of gifts within itself is a laudable and worthy human endeavor, but too often these gifts are mere swaps. They are given in the hope and expectation that they will be reciprocated, rather than as a heartfelt desire to give for the mere sake of giving.

But that is a phase of Christmas we need not consider. It is merely one small manifestation of the great forces that were set in motion on that Christmas morning 1927 years ago when Mother Mary wrapped her child in swaddling clothes and laid him in a manger—a feed trough for livestock—because "there was no room for them in the inn."

The incident of the manger is a prototype of the struggles and conquests of Christianity. It had lowly beginnings, and throughout history its stanchest supporters and heroes were of the common people. Christ spoke to the commoners; He was Himself a Commoner. Lacking an earthly kingdom, he set up a celestial empire in which everyone, rich and poor, shared alike.

He was the champion of the oppressed and downtrodden, the healer of wounds, the adjuster of injustices, the bringer of light, the destroyer of sin.

In Him centers all that is worthy in the race, past and present, and from Him flows all the good that men may do upon earth.

The empires conquered by such great leaders as Napoleon, Alexander, Cyrus and Attila have perished away, but the Empire established by the swordless carpenter boy of Nazareth will never perish. It is established forever upon the hills.

THE CHRISTMAS SPIRIT

December 23, 1928

Are we becoming wiser, or are we merely reaching a point where we are able to realize the hopelessness of pursuit, and are willing to become spectators rather than participants?

We speak of the mysterious something called the Christmas Spirit.

How many people have you heard say that they no longer have any joy in Christmas themselves, but find great pleasure in watching the children enjoy it? They recall their own childhood, and compare it with the childish display of eagerness and delight they see about them today. Unable to get any personal kick out of Christmas, they get a vicarious thrill in watching the children, or in giving to others.

That, after all, is a blessing and not a curse. This is the proper Christmas spirit—what the Good Book meant when it said that it is more blessed to give than to receive. The pleasure of receiving is wholly selfish. There is no happiness but in giving.

Some of us are wholly selfish, others merely less so. The world has seen but one truly unselfish man, and He was half God. We celebrate his birthday as a symbol of unselfishness to this day and will continute to celebrate for all time to come. He gave everything and received a crown of thorns. The cry of agony from the cross was not from a man who thought the world had failed to give him what he sought, but from a Deity who thought the world had refused to receive what he had given.

If we can reach the point where we grieve if we are unable to give, rather than mourn because we do not receive, we shall have drawn nigh enough unto Him to understand why He wept over Jerusalem—a Jerusalem that refused to receive the gift eternal.

There is something in the cry that Christmas has become commercialized, but the blame is not on the shoulders of the merchants. People nowadays give not for the pleasure of giving, but in the hope of receiving. There is a selfishness in their giving—the fear they will be thought "stingy" if they do not give, or the hope that they will get something of equal value in return.

That is the wrong spirit, but unfortunately it is the prevailing one. We are still human with all the human failings. We have not yet reached the height where we can give because we find a blessing in giving. That is, we have not reached the point as a people; we have in some individual circumstances. Until we do reach that point, our Christmas spirit will be lacking in its finer and only worthwhile element—the benediction of giving.

Cotton and Yuletide

December 19, 1929

One thing is certain as Christmas-tide approaches. The toy manufacturer's cost bill will be less than for several years.

We are indebted to Mr. T. J. Harrell of Fort Worth, president of the Texas Cottonseed Crushers Association, for the information that without the Texas cotton patch Santa Claus would be sadly handicapped in getting together the raw material for his workshop. Cotton is his principal dependence when toy-making time comes around; and cottonseed, of the same variety that grows on Texas farms, is the origin of nearly fifty of his products so dear to the hearts of children.

Taking her from the inside out, notes Mr. Harrell, the Christmas dolly is ninety per cent cotton. She is stuffed with linters. Her arms and legs, if they are celluloid, are partly made from cottonseed products. She is stitched together with cotton yarn, her synthetic silk dress and underwear, her artificial leather belt and the coating on the buckle, her felt hat and the dye stuff in her clothes and shoes, most likely had their beginnings

in the cotton patch. Even the varnish or lacquer on her
face, along with the twine used to wrap her for Christmas, and the paper in which she arrives, are products of
cotton.

Adds Mr. Harrell:

"Other toys and Christmas decoration, too, may
depend on cottonseed for their existence. The
waterproofing on rubber boots, insulating material on
toy electric trains and radios, films in Christmas Kodaks,
upholstery in all presents from the toy runabouts to
expensive automobiles, book bindings on literary gifts,
and even the writing paper on which Christmas greet-
ings are sent, had a common origin, probably on a Texas
farm.

"Cotton seed products, too, may be found in the
candles and candle wicks on the Christmas tree and in
the Christmas ornaments.

"Even Christmas music, jazz though it may be for
the younger generation, will come from phonograph
records containing cottonseed products.

"If mother catches Johnnie in time before he runs
in early Christmas morning to see his tree, he will be
washed with soap that probably contains cottonseed
foots.

"And after he has had his annual overdose of turkey
and candy, he will wind up a glorious Christmas with a

dose of emulsion—from the Texas cotton patch."

At this particular stage in the world's history royalty is having a rough time. Which may, after all, have some bearing on King Cotton's present down-at-the-heel condition.

Holiday Weather

December 20, 1929

There is nothing finer than a cold snap around Christmas time. The bullet-like rush of the icy north wind, while it cracks radiators and runs up the gas bill, is a great stimulator of jaded nerves. Also an aid to the

merchant who has hopefully stocked his shelves with Christmas goods.

It has always been thus, that a sudden change in the temperature—downward—amounts to nothing less than a psychological impulse on a people. It makes them step faster, think quicker, act with more decision. As a purse shaker it has no equal.

It also brings us into closer unity with Santa Claus. Somehow we could not put much heart in our welcome if the old gentleman appeared among us in his thick, red suit, mittens and heavy boots—on a warm, languid day.

For our happiness, for a closer appreciation of the joys of the Christmas season, let us hope the cold wave won't break until, at least the 26th of December.

SANTA'S GREAT SHOW

December 15, 1930

Santa Claus remains the biggest single drawing-card in Christendom, in spite of efforts to explode the old gentleman as a mere mythological character.

How else can you account for the perfectly astounding crowd of grown-ups and children who greeted Santa Claus and his parade in Abilene Saturday?

Lindbergh at his height of fame attracted a crowd approaching Santa's in size and enthusiasm. It was a tremendous crowd which met Lindy in Abilene, and they came from hundreds of miles around; but it wasn't as big as the crowd which Santa Claus and his show drew.

And it was the same everywhere in West Texas that Santa visited. Amarillo claimed 70,000 saw him there; San Angelo said it was a bigger crowd than attended the 1923 West Texas chamber of commerce convention in Angelo—and that was a crowd.

Only the finest sort of cooperation on the part of all agencies in this city—the municipal government, the chamber of commerce, the American Legion, the service clubs, the retail and wholesale merchants, the manufacturers, the fraternal orders, the schools and colleges—could bring out such a crowd and assure such a successful occasion. This newspaper, which brought Santa Claus to Abilene, is glad to have had a part in the demonstration, and proud of the way in which the citizenship cooperated to make it a success.

THE CHRISTMAS OF OUR CHILDHOOD

December 18, 1932

Enough has been written, heaven knows, about the various aspects of Christmas to fill a great many books. But there is one little phase of it that almost always seems to get overlooked—the strange, melancholy feeling of having somehow gone astray which is apt to beset almost every adult, in one way or another, as this holiday approaches.

It is a sort of combination, this feeling, of memory and disillusionment. Nobody ever says much about it, and the mood itself never lasts very long. But it is a real thing, haunting and disquieting, while it lasts.

The trouble, of course, is that none of us can feel quite the same about Christmas after we are fully grown as we felt when we were children.

For children, Christmas is by all odds the greatest day of the year. An air of excitement begins to pervade the world along about the end of the second week in December, and it approaches its crescendo with a mounting tension that is almost unbearable. The aura of promised wonders fills the air. Things long desired are about to be made real.

Then, on Christmas morning, comes the climax—green tree, glowing lights, squeals of excitement; are there, in all of life, any higher spots than a child gets during those first 30 minutes of Christmas morning?

The last week or so before Christmas brings memories of all of that into an adult's mind; and, try as he may, there is no way in which he can quite recapture that delightful old-time rapture and ecstasy. He can get a better appreciation of the real significance of the holiday, he can do his utmost to make the time a happy one for his own youngsters; but in the bottom of his heart there is bound to be a little void—the place, perhaps, occupied by the wraith of his own boyhood.

That void, to be sure, is always there. Our slow translation from innocence to wisdom, from childhood to manhood, leaves an empty spot we never can fill. But it is only at Christmas time that we have to think about it. And when we do we have to admit that neither the world in general nor we ourselves have ever quite fulfilled the gaudy promises that were explicit back in those far off days when the excitement of Christmas filled our hearts.

GRATEFUL

December 22, 1933

The spirit of Christmas is expressed in many ways, but a group of CWA workers engaged at the Fort Worth airport picked just about the niftiest way of expressing their gratitude that we have seen lately.

Contributing one penny apiece, the 150 men sent a telegram of thanks to President Roosevelt for having made it possible for them to work. They signed themselves "The Remembered Men."

The president gets about 1,500 fan letters a day, we are told, and it obviously would be impossible for him to read them all. It is a safe bet, however, that he read the telegram from Fort Worth.

Wonder how many people who have been helped in various ways by the Roosevelt New Deal have taken the trouble to write or wire him about it?

THE CHRISTMAS SPIRIT

December 18, 1934

Very few people fail to get a kick out of Christmas, and that is a very fine thing indeed; for existence is a rather drab and sheerless thing for most of us and even one emotional uplift a year is just so much gain.

The Christmas spirit is a very real factor in most human lives. It is not merely more blessed to give than to receive, but it offers a bigger spiritual reward. Happy is that man who has given happiness to someone else, especially to some child. We oldsters unfortunately have lost the child viewpoint about Christmas. We snort with indignation about the supposed commercialization of the event. But the child sees nothing commerial about it. He senses only that it is a time of special joy, a day or a few days of bright and particular happiness, when every-one is kind and gentle and anxious to see that he has everything he wants or should have.

So why not thaw out around Christmas time, and really let ourselves go? Emotionally and spiritually, we mean. In the worry and fret of the depressed years, we have contracted a sort of spiritual dry rot, an emotional drouth. We have been afraid to smile, almost, lest someone get the notion that all is well with us and go a-envying.

There are endless opportunities of getting a thrill out of Christmas. The obvious way is to remember your friends to the extent of your ability, if it is nothing more than a pat on the back. There is the Goodfellow fund and the Christmas seal sale and that family down the block who haven't been eating regularly. A little money goes a long way when it is given from the heart.

Why not "get that way" about Christmas? It really is our grandest institution.

THE LIGHTING PILGRIMAGE

December 14, 1937

One of the pleasures of the Christmas period is riding around town of evenings drinking in the beauties of the many lighting effects, some simple, some elaborate, spread before the public by participants in the Abilene Garden Club's annual lighting contest.

This year the number of contestants promises to be larger than usual, while the displays already in evidence indicate the competition will be keen. That means happy hunting for the motorist bent on seeing the sights.

The club is taking the practical step of outlining proposed tours for the seekers after beauty. Routes of travel will be given, so the motorist need not waste any time looking for the best displays.

It is a happy thought, one the citizenry should appreciate and take advantage of to the full. Watch for the routes of the club's Christmas lighting pilgrimage and follow them. They will give you a new appreciation of the club's activities and put you in a proper frame of mind to enjoy the Christmas holidays.

HITLER'S YULETIDE

December 16, 1939

It will be Christmas in Germany, too, this year. The "holiday season" has started in Berlin. But the air is acrid with gunpower, the music is a little off key, colored lights don't glimmer in the night, the song is not "Peace on Earth, Good Will to Men"—it is "Deutschland Uber Alles."

You may go shopping in Berlin department stores, but you probably can't buy that lavendar scarf for Gerhardt. It would take too many coupons out of the thin book that must last you a year. You may buy toys for little Oscar, but they will have to be swastika-trimmed tin soldiers or minature tanks and cannon. You may spread Christmas cheer if you have the money, coupons to spare, and the inclination to select from the meager array of gifts—all of which you probably haven't.

It is at a time like this when the irony of the Christmas lesson must ring the loudest. We still have peace, not on earth, but on our little corner of it. It is growing more precious every day. We should guard it carefully. It may become a collector's item.

SEASONAL THOUGHT

December 24, 1940

Up to this writing three of the Christmas cards that have come to us have been without signature or other indication as to the identity of the sender. We have not the heart to go too deeply into this subject, but all the same it has left us somewhat puzzled. Not that the identity of the unknown well-wishers is important, for good wishes are impersonal things and fall, like God's rain, on the just and the unjust at Christmastime. But we would like to know, out of sheer curiosity, why our correspondents failed or forgot to sign their names. Were they in too much of a hurry? Did they have something on their minds besides Christmas? Probably. But no matter; the thought was there, and if we can't make a mental note to remember them for their deed of kindness we can at least lump it under one general heading of lovingkindness and let it go at that.

There was a time when we considered Christmas cards silly and useless things, but as in many other cases we have changed our mind about it. It is true we never have gotten round to sending one, but knowing that we

39

had to learn to like oatmeal, bananas, spinach, cheese, foreigners and symphonic music, we daresay we'll get round to sending a Christmas card one of these days.

People have been sending us Christmas cards for years and years. The same people, we mean. And you have no idea of the cumulative effect of this gentle rain of rememberance. If one of these oldtimers ever forgets to remember us with a card at Christmas, it's going to spoil the whole thing for us. Like the time the river washed out the crops and Santa Claus just naturally didn't show up at all; not even a firecracker.

Some folks say the greeting card business is a sort of racket. For that matter some say Christmas is a racket too. But we can't string along with this viewpoint at all. Cards represent noble impulses, and you take noble impulses out of the world and what have you got left? Bombs and such stuff as totalitarians are made of.

The postman, rest his weary feet, may consider the spate of Christmas mail a device of the devil to harass honest folk; but if people didn't send mail to each other the postman wouldn't have a job, and there you are.

And we recipients of Christmas cards would feel sort of lost. We would imagine all sorts of things—whether the withholder had taken a dislike to us and our ways after all these years, whether he had died off, whether he had lost his last dime. You can see what a stir it would create in the breasts of us card receivers.

Come to think of it, we don't recall that we ever got round to thanking anybody for remembering us with a card at Christmas. Tck-tck. But we can't dwell on that thought, for it would sour us against ourself; and at Christmas time one should be kind even to one's self, the hardest individual on earth to get along with.

So to one and all—card senders, whether signed or unsigned; people who meant to send a card but forgot it at the last moment; and everybody else within the sound of our typewriter, thanks.

WE'VE HAD OUR SHARE OF LUCK

December 24, 1942

Santa Claus has been good to the United Nations, and some of his greatest gifts just became public knowledge within the last few weeks.

Winston Churchill made known one gift, when he reported that after the fall of France, Britain was left with only 100 tanks of a type found practically useless in fighting on the continent. Had Hitler struck at the islands at that moment he would have found them all but defenseless. The best divisions in the British Army had been crushed and demoralized, escaping at Dunkerque only by what seemed a miracle.

The lowdown seems to be that France fell unexpectedly soon, and Hitler had no plans for immediate invasion of England. He also counted on the British suing for peace, forgetting that Englishmen are even more stubborn than the Dutch. Upshot was that Hitler idled for months when he might have wiped the islands off the map—which would be the only way to subdue them.

Secretary Knox has told us how near we came to losing the war in the Pacific before it was fairly started. The Japs struck us a harder blow at Pearl Harbor than they imagined, sinking or crippling a full half of our battleships. Had they been prepared to occupy the islands there is little doubt they would have succeeded. But they were not prepared for that—they had intended Pearl Harbor as merely a crippling blow, to give them time to take Hong Kong, Singapore, Java and the Philippines.

Whether these axis blunders were the products of stupidity or the dispensation of Divine Providence is any man's guess. Probably a bit of both. But they constituted handsome Christmas presents for the United Nations all the same. They saved the day for us.

No Room—Anywhere

December 13, 1943

Most of us are intent on getting somebody a suitable Christmas present, or trying to figure out what somebody is going to give us. Few of us stop to think, or even know, that this custom probably stems from the gifts which the Magi placed at the feet of Mary and her child at Bethlehem.

"O little town of Bethlehem, how still we see thee lie!" If we had only been a resident of that village 1943 years ago, and the Holy Family had come seeking accommodations, and there was no room in the inn—how gladly we would have thrown open our spare bedroom!

Is that so! Listen, last Saturday morning a frail little mother with her infant in her arms was walking wearily along South First street, near the high school. She had been out in the inclement weather, trying in vain to find a room for herself and child. She was just about all in.

Oh, sure it was foolish of her to come to this overcrowded city to be with her soldier husband. Utterly illogical. But whoever said love was a logical thing, in the first place? It is the only brand of insanity that is sweet. It was foolish of Joseph to take Mary to Bethlehem in her condition, too—if you want to be crassly logical instead of humanly understanding.

There was no room in the inn. Well, at least none "available." And don't say, after 2,000 years of Christian civilization, that the Bethlehemites were a stupid and selfish and stone-hearted lot, and it would have been different if you'd been there. Who knows?—that cold little baby shivering in its mother's arms while she walked our streets looking for a place to stay may grow up to be a great religious leader, or statesman, or scien-

tist—if indifference doesn't kill him first. Who knows?—maybe the scroll of Time has been rolled back 1943 years and this is just another moment of census-taking.

Did not the Infant say, Lo, I am with you alway? Did He not say, I was a stranger, and ye took me in? Did He not say, Inasmuch as ye have done it unto one of the least of these my brethren, ye have done it unto me?

GIFT SUGGESTIONS

December 18, 1943

During the past few weeks we have been besieged by relatives and friends with requests that we suggest a few trinkets we would enjoy receiving for Christmas. Such demands now are rising to an almost shrill crescendo.

This is embarrassing. True, we do not have everything that we want. The car is getting shabby, and surely we could use a set of new tires (five, please, if you like this idea). The keys on our typewriter are a bit out of alignment, but we've got rather fond of the old mill, so perhaps we'll pass that up.

There are a few other things that come to mind. For instance, next spring we shall be in the market for some two-leather sport shoes, preferably alligator bottoms and white tops, for which no coupon is in sight even if two-colored shoes weren't off the market.

These and similar wants, unfortunately, may not appeal to our relatives and friends, or may prove hard to find in the stores.

In that case we have a couple of other ideas from current advertisements which should offer no difficulties.

A New York-Beverly Hills haberdasher has a hand-painted tie, which in the illustration looks like one of those pillows one wins at a county fair by tossing rings over pins. It is unique. Only one of a kind is made. If you give us that, nobody in the whole wide world will have a tie like ours, and we are certain that all who see us in it will gasp, at the very least, and will always remember the occasion, and us.

One of these ties can be purchased for as little as $25, although for $50 and up it is possible to obtain better art works and, presumably, a higher grade of pigment in the paints used.

From the catalog of the Greatest Sporting Goods Store in the World we learn that deluxe English cigaret lighters are available for either dress or daily use. They possess imported Swiss mechanisms. The 14-karat gold case is engine-turned, and comes in a variety of designs. There is space for monograming on top.

The ladies' model, including tax, costs only $137.50. But this is not for us. There is a gentleman's model, on which also the tax has been figured in, for $148.50.

Incidentally, we have been asked to suggest something that would please the Little Woman. That has been a sticker, but the other day we watched her poring spellbound over the advertisement of a Fifth Avenue (New York) store, wherein was contained a dignified announcement that one Arnaud (to paraphrase the name) is available for interviews.

We quote from the discreet little notice, which was headed "the Arnaud Hour."

"In the privacy of a studio, Arnaud will study your features and personality . . . he will give consultation lessons to his clients . . . he will create individual coiffeurs from the informal to the most glamorous . . . he will make an exciting, drastic change in your looks and personality. Appointment by letter only. 50.00 an hour." (No sordid dollar sign, please note. This appeal is to persons of refinement and delicacy.)

Arnaud, we understand, does not cut hair or wave it or do anything like that. Not, at least, in person during the Arnaud Hour. His services are more cultural and inspirational. It is his function to tell our wives how they can become new women, exciting women, glamorous women—women who will make their husbands feel almost like unintentional bigamists.

There are suggestions for the family. We hope you like them.

When It Comes to Christmas

December 23, 1943

Christmas is our finest day. Although most of us are given to rude display of wealth (as represented by gifts costlier than we can afford) we get nearer to genuine unselfishness on this than on any other day.

We are a sentimental people, a fact of which we should not be in the least ashamed, although some of us would rather be overtaken in a crooked business deal or a bit of unethical conduct than be caught doing something that might be construed as sentimental. That is, on all occasions except Christmas. At Christmas we get as sentimental as all git-out and we don't give a whoop who knows it. It's the one day of the year a strong man can get as sloshy and mushy as a schoolgirl without being considered a sissy. One of the most moving sights we witnessed this Christmas week was a shopping expedition made up of stalwart men in uniform, gathering decorations for their outfit's Christmas tree. Being incurably sentimental, we choked up suddenly and had to get out of there—and it wasn't with laughter, either.

So we applaud our Uncle Sam for his determination to spread what Christmas cheer he can among his nephews fighting in the far corners of the world. By ship and plane gift packages have been delivered to pin-point islands in the Pacific, to frozen-in outposts in the Aleutians, to Jap-beset patrols in Bougainville and New Britain, to ships at sea, to the fighting lines in Italy. Nobody but a fool would begrudge the shipping space taken up by these packages from home; they are more precious than rubies and greater morale-builders than a battle won. Many a grimy doughboy or overworked medic or sky-splitting pilot will gather around an impromptu Christmas tree Friday night and get the first sense of home he has had in many a long month.

For we are all kids when it comes to Christmas— and if you don't like it you can jolly well take a long running jump. And we're all the better for being that way.

For with all its faults Christmas is a manifestation of that universal love which Christ showered upon all mankind, without regard to race, color, creed or previous conditions. It is quite true that we have overcommericalized it and abused it and held it lightly, but Christmas still means more to more of God's children than anything else in life.

Yes, even in the midst of carnage mankind takes a little time out to dwell with loving thoughts on what might have been. If he could only spread the spirit of Christmas over the other 364 days of the year, what a joyous place this old earth would be!

Half a loaf is better than no bread, so let us make the most of Christmas and be thankful for the opportunity.

FACE TO FACE

December 27, 1943

It was a quiet Christmas in Europe's war zone. By tacit common consent both sides knocked off the killing for the day and celebrated the birthday of the Gentle Nazarene in their own ways.

Some people expressed astonishment at this. Both sides had refused all pleas for a Christmas armistice, and it was said Hitler had planned an invasion on that day. The weather was ideal for it; nevertheless the day passed quietly.

But history has a way of repeating itself. By common consent in many wars involving so-called Christian nations Christmas brought a cessation of killing. Troops facing each other across a no man's land of hate dropped their weapons and fraternized. They exchanged presents of cigarets and candy. That is, they did until their officers broke it up, for men who are trained to kill each other on sight can't be allowed to get soft.

It is a curious fact that there is less hate at the battlefront than in civil areas. This is an unbelievable thing to most people, but not to men who have actually been in battle. They would have a hard time explaining it, but there it is, as real as life itself.

Kipling expressed it pretty well in his Ballad of East and West. There is no border, breed nor birth when two strong men come face to face though they come from the ends of the earth. Fighting men seldom if ever start wars; they merely fight them. It remains for the noble statesmen at home to mess things up and get soldiers to fighting each other; and it remains for us people safe and comfortable in our homes and at our fireside to do a real first class job of hating. God forgive us.

A soldier's death in battle is the noblest of all, not because war is noble but because the soldier's death is unselfish. As Tennyson put it, His not to reason why, his but to do and die. The statesmen do the reasoning why, and almost invariably they come up with the wrong answer.

THE FIRST GOODFELLOW

December 13, 1944

With Christmas less than two weeks away the Goodfellows aren't doing so well. Only a little more than a third of the needed $2,000 had been contributed up to yesterday.

The poor we have with us always. The breadwinner gets sick, or breaks a leg. Misfortune overtakes the family in a dozen different ways. Then there is always the family which doesn't earn more than enough to keep soul and body together. Not everybody is making whopping big wages these days. Perhaps the breadwinner doesn't work hard enough, doesn't see after his family as he should. Quite possibly he is a no-account. But what about the kids? Is that their fault?

Nothing on this earth is like a cheerless Christmas.

There needn't be a cheerless home in Abilene this Christmas if the Goodfellows come through. They always have come through, but we here at the office are getting just a little uneasy this time.

Anybody can become a Goodfellow simply by kicking in with whatever he feels like giving. Some of the Old Faithfuls have been doing it for 25 years. They wouldn't miss the chance for anything.

Nobody's going to be high-pressured. The Goodfellows don't do business that way. It's strictly voluntary. They give because they want to give, because they know in their hearts what a great thing it is to make someone else happy at Christmas.

Many of the Goodfellows got that way because they missed a Christmas or two themselves, and know what it means.

It is one of life's bitterest experiences.

"And they brought young children to him, that he should touch them; and his disciples rebuked those that brought them. But when Jesus saw it, he was much displeased, and said unto them, Suffer the little children to come unto me, and forbid them not; for of such is the kingdom of God."

He was the first Goodfellow.

IT ISN'T CHRISTMAS ANY MORE

December 26, 1944

They tell us that Christmas isn't like it used to be, and perhaps they are right; for we seem to sense a change in the Christmas spirit that contrasts unfavorably with the Yuletide of our boyhood. There has been a shift in values, it seems to us, and not for the better either.

For those of us who were born with a wooden spoon in our mouths, back in the 1890s and beyond, our wishes were modest and our joys were simple and unaffected. If we got an apple, an orange, a few assorted nuts, a stick of striped candy and—wonder of wonders—a cheap tin or wooden toy in our Christmas stocking, our happiness was unbounded. If, as often happened, the family fortunes were at a low ebb and there wasn't anything but an apple or an orange in the old sock, if that much, we took it in our stride—Santa Claus was too busy carrying things to all the other little boys and girls in the world to pay us a call.

If the family fortunes were on the upgrade, there might be a few Roman candles, a few packages of Chinese firecrackers, some pinwheels and possibly a skyrocket in each little individual's pile of Christmas things.

We don't seem to remember there was any difference in the measure of our joy whether there was much or little; it was only when there was nothing that it hurt.

That was when we made the discovery that the community ne'er-do-well, who played poker for money, drank everything he could lay hands on, and was suspected of preferring the company of his foxhounds to that of human beings—that was when we found who had the biggest heart in our little broad place in the road. It was none other; for he alone sensed that there were

empty stockings to be filled, and like young Lochinvar riding out of the West, he rode by and filled them.

The modern Christmas has pretty well broken loose from the anchor of its original concept. It has become commercialized out of all semblance to the real thing, and this is a great pity. It has lost its simplicity and underlying spirit of giving for joy's sake rather than for the gift's sake. And slowly but surely we are beginning to hate and deplore it.

Trying Christmases

December 24, 1945

Though peace on earth may be new and precarious, and good will may be of doubtful measure, this should be a Merry Christmas for most of us. This is not the year to rejoice with reservation, for there are too many who deserve to celebrate the day with whole-hearted joy.

If there are any who have a happy holiday with accrued interest coming to them, it's the kids who have had to put up with a lot from a badly managed adult world these last few years.

Wartime Christmases have been particularly trying for the older generation of small fry whose memories go back beyond Pearl Harbor. They remember days when bicycles, skates and electric trains and sturdy metal trucks and fire engines, all of them new and shining, were to be found beneath the tree. They have been remarkably patient with ersatz substitutes and it's time they had something better, even though Santa Claus hasn't been able to reconvert completely to peacetime production.

Wartime Christmases must have been incomplete and bewildering to thousands of the smaller youngsters. They've needed a father around holiday time who was something more than a picture on the table, or a vaguely remembered person who was too far away and too busy fighting the war even to hook a ride with Santa and arrive on Christmas Eve. And needless to say it has been tough on their absent fathers, and on the mothers who tried to do double parental duty with half a heart.

But the wartime Christmases are past. Many of those fathers already are home, and many more even now are on the last lap of the journey that will bring them back in time for the reunion that is the best and most treasured gift of all.

They will find no quarrel with the day's perfection, and the rest of us might take our cue from them. There is trouble and sorrow in the world, as always. But concerned though we may be, our concern should not intrude upon this celebration crowned at last with victory and peace.

And so, a Merry Christmas to all.

NOEL, NOEL

December 19, 1946

It seems wicked to throw a damper on Santa Claus, but considering that every American man, woman and child owes something like $2,000 apiece on the nation's war debt, the Christmas spending splurge seems more than slightly cockeyed.

An Associated Press roundup tells us that Christmas spending in Texas is really something, and presumably the same holds true of the nation. The plus percentage in sales volume looks like the results of a high-scoring basketball game between two fast offensive teams. The poor postal workers are catching Hail, Columbia, Happy Land in large doses. Salespeople wear that harried, Oh-how-my-feet-hurt look in their eyes. Hapless males delegated to carry bundles through the jostling throngs resemble Mexican burros burdened with firewood.

The veracious AP, cheerful soul, records that people aren't snatching at stuff as they did a year ago, but are actually taking quality and value into consideration. Is that a fact, now! Enough hard cash is spent on a single Christmas gift to ransom a king—or to keep the donor in room and board for years if Hard Times ever return.

One hates to be a sourpuss amidst such overwhelming evidence of happiness and the glad, free joy of giving; but is there no Tomorrow, no Day After? Remember those insurance premiums? Remember the income tax man? Remember the bill collector?

Who remembers when a simple toy and a stocking-full of red apples and bright oranges sufficed the child? Who remembers when just having one's loved ones and

friends around made Christmas a joyous occasion, full of warmth and beauty?

Today Christmas is an anti-climax, a letdown from a mad rush of preparation, and a three-ply pain in the neck. Nobody is satisfied with simple things any more. We have wrung the last drop of anticipatory bliss from the occasion, and what we have left is a slightly tarnished, sordid-seeming something or other. Who shot Santa Claus?

Hark, the Angels

December 9, 1947

In Brooklyn a rather hefty controversy is raging over the action of the supervisor of about thirty public schools in ordering an end to the singing of Christmas carols by school kids. There were immediate protests from Christian groups and others, but at last account the embattled school supervisor was standing his ground. The higher school authorities were doing a Pilate—they were washing their hands of the affair, on the ground that the decision was within the discretion of the local official in charge.

Particularly objected to was "Hark the Herald Angels Sing." Adding to the delicacy of the situation was the fact that about 20,000 of the 30,000 pupils in the schools affected were Jewish, the others Christians of various sects.

It had never occurred to us that Christmas and its songs, its symbols and above all its spirit had anything but a universal and non-sectarian implication and appeal. Certainly in a commercial sense all sects have made use of the occasion for pecuniary gain. It would seem that the best interests of the business community, especially in an enormous place like New York, would best be served by slapping down any attempt to channelize or circumscribe the observance of Christmas.

No test for musical appreciation, to our knowledge, was ever given to the receivers or the givers of Christmas cheer. Christmas has long been a sort of neutral strip in the vast expanse of human relationships, often quite acrimonious and riotous among the different religions. Christmas is the one time of the year when everbody gets nearest to being "as a little child."

We would hate to be the man who shot Santa Claus with the hair-trigger pistol of prejudice and misunderstanding. It isn't the words that count with Christmas carols: it's the spirit behind the words and the music. It's the spirit of the occasion—peace on earth, good will to men.

Northern magazines and commentators are full of the subject of racial antagonisms in the South. They can't see the forest for the trees. There is more racial antagonism visible in New York and environs than anywhere else in the country.

CHRISTMAS CANDLES

December 22, 1947

The use of candles at Christmas time is said to come down to modern times from the days of the Roman Emperor Constantine for whom Byzantium was renamed Constantinople when he transferred the capital of the empire there. Constantine converted to Christianity after seeing a luminous cross in the sky, introduced the ritual of the lighted candle into Christian services of worship, and ordered special illumination on Christmas Eve.

Today there are all kinds and shapes of Christmas candles: Santa Claus waxen images, snow men, bells and snow balls, not to mention the more orthodox tapers in white and red. These may seem a far cry from the days of Constantine who lived in the fourth century A.D. Nevertheless when we light a candle at Christmas time—and who doesn't?—we are following a pattern that this Roman emperor started.

Lights on the tree also come from an old Norse practice of hanging bright baubles on an evergreen tree at the period of greatest darkness, to show the gods that men wanted the world to look bright again with the trees green and the fruits and blossoms gay.

The likeness in customs of different peoples is a strange thing. Perhaps it will help in the end to further the thinking of people that humanity and the world are one.

NIGHT'S LODGING

December 23, 1947

There is a lot of Christmas abroad in the land at this time, but the big question is, How much of Christ is there in Christmas the way we celebrate it?

Suppose a man and his wife, riding in a rickety-rattling jalopy, drove into this town Wednesday evening,

having been summoned to answer a traffic violation ticket for cutting a corner. The man is obviously poor in this world's goods. His face wears a worried look, for his wife is far gone with child, and they have been turned away at every hotel and rooming house in the city. Maybe there really was "no room for them in the inn," but it is altogether possible the proprietor doubted this poor couple's ability to pay their bill. Besides, he didn't want a baby squalling all over the place.

If the worried husband knocked at your door and asked for a night's accommodation, what would your answer be? Your house is all a-light with Christmas decorations. There is a tree in the corner of the living room, its foot surrounded by bright packages. There is merriment in the house, and a vast contentment. On the morrow the packages will be opened, and hearts will be high. On this eve of Christmas it would be extremely annoying to have a thinly-clad stranger knock on the door and ask to spend the night.

So if you were an average householder, your answer would be short and sharp. "See the Salvation Army," or maybe United Charities.

It is easy to be the kind of Christian a great many people are. It takes real courage and love of humanity to be the kind of Christian the followers of the Babe of Bethlehem are supposed to be.

Christmas constitutes our greatest testing-time. Circumstances being what they are, human frailty being what it is, we are very much afraid any couple named Joseph and Mary, with a baby due any minute, might have to knock on many doors before being invited to spend the night even in a chicken coop.

The Gift of the Magi

December 22, 1948

In a roundabout way, but from reliable sources, we came across a little human interest story the other day that renewed our faith in Santa Claus in particular and the essential goodness of most people in general.

We feel sure the participants in this little drama of Christmas good followship won't mind our passing the story along, so here goes:

Anybody who was raised in a parsonage can tell you that there are times when the larder gets pretty bare, and that often when things look darkest it is refilled so unexpectedly as to seem miraculous.

New ministerial students especially have to struggle to make ends meet. There are thousands of them in this country, and their wives, who make great sacrifices and endure many hardships in order to complete their education.

The hero of our Christmas story has been "pastoring" a little country church fifty miles or so from his college, to gain practical experience and to help take care of his wife and two children.

One day recently the little family discovered the cupboard was bare. The husband and father had only a few cents in his pocket. It looked like a bleak, not to mention, a hungry, Christmas for them all.

But the young head of the household was full of faith.

"Something will turn up," he assured his young wife. "You just wait and see."

At that moment there was a knock on the front door. It was a neighbor, with a big fat hen in his hand. "Thought you folks might like a little change in diet,"

said the man, thrusting the hen into the parson's hand. Then the Good Samaritan left hurriedly.

The wife was still wiping her eyes, when an automobile honked outside. The little family rushed out to see what was up. It was a member of their church, a man who doesn't go to church often, and who makes no bones about taking a drink now and then. In his car was a two or three weeks' supply of groceries for the parsonage. Compliments of Santa Claus.

Well, that's about all there is to our Christmas story, except that when the parson's wife opened one of the cartons of eggs a little later, she found a crisp twenty-dollar United States bill inside.

The Oldtime Christmas

December 23, 1948

More than one oldtimer bewails the disappearance of the old-fashioned family Christmas, but there doesn't seem to be much anyone can do about bringing it back.

Instead of staying home for Christmas as was the almost universal custom half a century ago, everybody either goes visiting or has in a lot of company. Football games and other diversions tend to break up family groups, and send individual members in all directions from the family fireside.

In the old days the community Christmas tree, usually set up at the schoolhouse, was a bushy cedar brought in from the hills and trimmed with homemade decorations. There would be a program, with little boys and girls "reciting" or singing carols. A sure-enough, bona-fide Santa Claus would come bustling in to read off the names on the presents, and to kid everybody.

The presents leaned heavily to colored candy, firecrackers and apples and oranges. Toys were few and far between, because it took cash to buy toys and there was very little hard money in the community. Yet everybody lived well and was happy.

In the home, everybody hung his stocking on the mantel and found it full of candy, nuts, oranges and apples next morning. Surprise!

Mother and the girls had spent a week cooking Christmas pies and cakes, and a fat turkey with plenty of dressing formed the piece de resistance.

Everybody went around yelling "Christmas gift!" at everybody else, trying to get in the word first. Some of the greedy ones jumped the gun the day before by shouting: "Christmas Eve gift!"

We hope the modern kids enjoy Christmas like we used to, but we have our doubts. Most of them have become surfeited.

MAGIC LITTLE SEALS

December 14, 1949

Somewhere on this cluttered desk is an envelope addressed to the Taylor County Tuberculosis Association, Box 590, Abilene, Texas. Must fill out a check and mail it in to cover those Christmas Seals. Should have done it weeks ago. Procrastination is the thief of time; also, better late than never.

Somebody has handed us a few so-called dry statistics. This year 9,614 Taylor County residents took the free X-ray test for t.b. Of these, 194 showed suspicious evidence of having had a tubercular infection. Of these, 155 were rather definite old tuberculars (cured up now, thank heavens), and only 39 were listed as "suspicious" as of time of examination.

Well, those tidy little Christmas Seals made possible these 9,614 X-rayed chests in Taylor County, and thousands of others like them throughout the state.

By having had warning in time, those 39 suspicious chests need not despair; indeed proper treatment should fix them up for long, useful and carefree lives; for t.b. is readily curable if discovered in time.

That is where the little Christmas Seals come in, but that isn't all they do; they help to care for the ones who are in the incipient stages, and for those who have discovered their plight almost too late, and for those who discovered their plight entirely too late.

You hardly ever hear the once-familiar term, "The Great White Plague," any more. It is still with us, but it isn't the terror it once was.

The little Christmas Seals are largely responsible for reducing tuberculosis from the status of a plague to that of a more or less minor infection—if discovered in time and promptly treated.

If you didn't happen to get the little seals in the mail, send a check to Box 590 anyhow. It will be needed, and it will do a world of good. It will give you that warm, Christmassy glow, too.

Only Three More Days

December 21, 1949

Three more days to Christmas. Time is running out on the sluggards and the postponers, the procrastinators and the undecided. A purchase in time saves frazzled nerves and uncertain tempers. That old last-minute rush imposes hardships on everybody—salespeople, wrappers, postoffice employes and postmen especially. Shop early in the morning if you can. Decide what you want and go after it. Don't take up the salespeople's time trying to make up your mind at the last minute. They are working overtime this week, and will be fit to be tied by closing time Saturday.

By and large, from all accounts, Christmas buying has been pretty brisk. The fear that there might be a big buying letdown this Christmas hasn't seemed to materialize. In the nation as a whole, buying was expected to be off five to ten percent from last year. In some parts of the country, notably wherever John L. Lewis' miners live, the decrease must be considerable. In some industrial areas where full employment has not yet been achieved since last spring and summer's letdown, business has been none too brisk.

But in our own part of the country, where oil and agriculture rule the roost, it's been pretty good. Everybody who really wants to work has been busy. The cotton crop was a whopper, and the cotton pickers were in clover even if the cotton farmer's overhead ate up much of his potential profit.

The oil boom helped practically everybody, first and last. It gave employment to thousands. It helped

landowners and merchants. In spite of cut-back production, the industry gave Texas a big break because of the
extraordinary amount of drilling and wildcatting that is
going on. If Santa Claus wore a slicker and a tin hat,
he'd be recognized almost anywhere in Texas. The oil
field roughneck symbolizes the old boy pretty well.

It's been a great year. We have nothing to complain
of. Just get your shopping done and r'ar back and enjoy
the holidays.

SANTA CLAUS ROUGHED UP

December 11, 1950

We are beginning to get a little bit suspicious of this Santa Claus business. Some of his managers and sponsors are getting far too cute to suit our taste.

Maybe this is why old Santy has been assaulted recently in such widely separated places as a town in Illinois and city in Germany. In Illinois, a bunch of high school students snowballed Santa as he rode down the street in a Christmas parade, knocking off his headgear and seriously impairing his dignity.

In the German city, the kids actually set fire to Kris Kringle's clothes, and the old boy blazed up brightly. Quick-acting townspeople put the old fellow out by rolling him in the snow. He was singed, and we suspect, lost some of his tradional love for the dear little oafs. Donner-wetter!

But the cuteness we referred to was at Lock Haven, Pa. A business man's Santa Claus committee had planned to dress up one of its members, drive him to nearby Williamsport, put him aboard a plane there and bring him in for a lively landing at Lock Haven. But the weather interfered, so Santa was taken to one end of the Lock Haven airport, put aboard a plane, which circled the field a couple of times and made a perfect landing while the assembled kiddies cheered wildly—unaware of the deception. It says here.

Oh, well; any port in a storm. We suppose the Lock Haven business men are proud of themselves for delivering Santa Claus as promised, even if it did take a bit of doing.

But a few more incidents of the kind and it's going to be hard to keep us children fooled about Santa Claus. Well do we remember the time when, at age five, we peeked from under the covers and caught Santa at his work minus every semblance of facial spinach except a bristly mustache au naturel. That was when the deceivers became the deceived, for in a burst of selfish enlightment we decided to lie doggo and say nothing. It worked. Thereafter, until age ten, we never so much as peeked from under the covers again.

No use letting the grownups get wise to how hard we kiddies are to fool.

Spirit of the Occasion

December 7, 1951

Everybody has at least one Christmas he remembers more vividly than any other, and it is sometimes pleasant and profitable to recall those bright moments out of the past, and to contemplate with awe the marvel-

ous faculty which enables us to remember things that happened long, long ago.

The one we recall most vividly was fifty years ago. The kids were all bundled up snugly against winter's chill—a crisp, clear day it was—and packed into the back of the flat-bed wagon, with Pa on the spring seat driving, and Ma beside him hunkered against the cold. We were going to Aunt Mary's for Christmas, and the distance was only a few miles. We were making a lot of racket, as kids will especially around Christmas, and every now and then Pa would turn around with a fierce expression on his face and say, "I don't want to have to speak to you children again!" This alternation of racket and lecture kept up the whole way to Aunt Mary's—a moment of quiet after each admonition, soon to be broken by a fresh outburst of laughter and yells of sheer enjoyment.

We don't recall any specific Christmas present handed out—probably the usual apple, orange and candy in the usual black ribbed cotton stocking. What we do remember is the spirit of the occasion, the moods of the moment, the nameless little thrills we always associate with Christmas.

We oldsters may recapture these moments of bliss only in retrospect. We are reminded of them by the happy laughter and antics of children around us, and we praise God for the memories of childhood which they awaken in us.

Well, we are some older now physically, and we worry about the condition of our remaining teeth, and wonder when our dentist is going to say, "Let's just cut out this foolishness and have 'em out," and our joints need oiling and it's a little difficult to get up in the morning, but as long as we can recapture even in hazy outline some of those childhood Christmases we're not going to be resentful and fearful of the creeping years, but just turn loose all holds and enjoy ourself come Christmas.

CHRISTMAS TREE LORE

December 13, 1951

Forty or fifty years ago the Texas family intent on putting up a Christmas tree would hie into the hills and knock over a cedar. Some still do that as a matter of tradition, but most trees are store-bought and prices have become something fierce.

Christmas trees is now big business. They are grown systematically for the purpose they are intended to serve. Trees of the proper symmetrical proportions don't grow in quantity in a wild state; most marketable Christmas trees are cultivated. Franklin D. Roosevelt was almost a pioneer in this business, and his son Elliott is carrying on the crop.

Using a Christmas tree is a fairly recent thing in America. It spread from Scandinavia and Germany into England, thence into the U.S. The first record of a Christmas tree in this country dates only from 1834 in Philadelphia and from 1835 in Cincinnati. Germans put them both up.

The centerpiece of any Christmas celebration prior to the advent of the decorated tree was the yule log,

called also block or clog. Our mother used to tell us how
the slaves would search for weeks to find the biggest log
they could handle, and then soak it on the sly for several
more weeks in a pond or creek to make it more fire
resistant. The log was rolled into the fireplace Christmas
Eve, and as long as there was any part of it left to burn,
the slaves were free from any labor except routine
chores, hence the elaborate precautions to get a long-
burning log.

Christmas itself was in bad odor among the Puritans. Oliver Cromwell caused a law to be enacted during his reign penalizing any celebration of Christmas, and ordered all shops to stay open for business as usual. Until well up into this century some ultra-Puritanical preachers denounced the decoration of a Christmas tree as sinful.

Many men, many minds. Many nowadays decry the commercialization of the holy day, but it looks as though Santa Claus is here to stay.

HARK THE HERALD ANGELS

December 14, 1951

A pleasant old Yuletide custom of other years has all but disappeared from our ken, and the people are poorer for its passing. We speak of carol-singing by groups of young people going from door to door on Christmas eve, singing carols many of which dated back to our remote Anglo-Saxon traditions.

Now and then at Christmastime we have seen this old custom revived here, but it never seemed to be on an organized basis, and the groups of singers have been small and not covering much territory.

In the smaller towns in the old days the boys and girls, young men and women, were out early and singing late, their fresh young voices rising clear and far-carrying on the chilly night air. One household would meet them with hot coffee and cakes, another would pass around candy, still others simply applauded and expressed thanks.

Whether the singers received a handout or merely thanks, or not even thanks, they gave their best and their effort paid off in its own coin — the coin not measured in cold figures, but in an uplift of the spirit.

Like old wine, the old carols are best. They fit and express the Christmas spirit as nothing else can. Untold generations of English-speaking peoples have sung them or heard them sung, and were all the better for it.

We suppose we are hopelessly old-fashioned, given too much to reminiscence and sentimental backward-looking, but when the custom of carol-singing at Christmas was allowed to lapse by a materialistic, practical and unsentimental modern society, something fine and noble went out of our Yuletide celebration, and nothing approaching it in form and substance was created in its place.

We can hear them yet—the eager, earnest young voices, singing songs their remote ancestors sung, in the same words, precisely the same cadence, and with the same heartfelt feeling, standing in a circle in front of the house in the chill evening, as much a part of Christmas as Santa Claus.

POST-CHRISTMAS ITEMS

December 27, 1951

Ham Wright's hog-killing story in our Christmas edition must have brought back some pleasant memories to a lot of us senior citizens. Those were the days down on the farm, and the younger generations don't know what they missed. We checked with Ham on a couple of items he failed to mention, a matter that used to create quite a rivalry among the boys who were always eager helpers at hog-killing time, but usually just getting in the way. One was the privilege of stripping the hair off the hog's tail after it had been properly scalded in the tilted barrel. The other was to gain possession of the bladder and blow it up into a very satisfactory balloon, much like those given away now for advertisement purposes. The little girls shied away from both these by-products of hog-killing, considered them inelegant or something, but the boys esteemed them very highly indeed. We can smell that good old sausage and red-eyed gravy to this day . . .

By Saturday or maybe a little later, Dad will get tired playing with the Christmas gadgets and give Junior

94

a chance to try his hand. Cheer up, Junior, it's just
passing fancy with Dad, and he will get over it in due
time and give you a chance. Dads seem to fool with
electric trains longer than any other gadget, but some of
these toy automobiles that wind up and go whoosh are
almost irresistible. We've got calluses on our thumb and
forefinger . . .

Our gifts of Christmas ties increased 300 percent
this year, from last year's one to 1951's three. At the risk
of committing heresy, we'd like to say that all our ties
were pretty and we appreciated them as a contribution

to a good cause. We change our socks daily, but hardly ever get around to changing a necktie. Now that our supply has been replenished, we figure to get extravagant and change ties every two or three weeks. By making changes frequently, we hope to get through 1952 with our present supply of ties, without having to buy any more. Retrenchment will be the order of the day at our house, in view of higher and higher taxes.

THE WEEK IN BETWEEN

December 26, 1952

Exactly one week after Christmas comes New Year's Day, and the period in between is shot through with cleaning up after one celebration to make way for the next.

The post-Christmas letdown in the stores isn't as noticeable as you might think, after the frantic weeks of the Christmas shopping season. There is always a big mess to clean up, customers with gifts to exchange, and a general rearrangement and overhaul of stock to take care of—with your feet absolutely killing you from the long and rushing hours preceding Christmas.

Everybody somehow manages to get through the week lying between Christmas and New Year's, but it is always a strange, unreal sort of time in everyone's life, unlike any other week of the year.

In most households the Christmas decorations are allowed to stay up, for want of sufficient energy to take them down. After all, why not? If you have done your work well with them, they stay pretty a long time, and you might as well get the enjoyment of them as long as possible.

If there are children in the household, you might as well resign yourself to a period of dodging toys on the floor, putting aside your customary reading to read from childish books, separating combatants who fall to blows over the possession of some plaything, dosing youself for the ills of over-eating and perhaps over-drinking, and otherwise making yourself useful if not ornamental.

Try as you will, you cannot quite shut out the fact that 1953 is approaching with all its problems of tax-paying, auto licensing, and a thousand and one other problems a switch in years entails.

If you have bought overgenerously and excessively of Christmas presents, there are bills to consider, corners to cut, postponings to be arranged and deals to be engineered.

But you try to put these distressing matters out of your mind in the week between the two great holidays, and cultivate the processes of recovery from the most strenuous of them, the so-called Yuletide.

Chances are your feet hurt, perhaps your head aches, certainly you have butterflies in your stomach from overindulging. But cheer up. It's 364 days to Christmas.

Coma Ti Yi Yippy

December 15, 1953

The Christmas card of Fay and Boyce House this year consists of quotations from "The Old Chisholm Trail," a reflection of Boyce House's absorption in the subject of Texas and its lighter sides. It brings up that old refrain: "Coma ti yi yippy, yippy-a, yippy-a. Coma ti yi yippy, yippa-a, yippy-a!"

"Oh, I had a ten-dollar hoss and a forty-dollar saddle. And I started up the trail just a punching Texas cattle."

Well, the drovers encountered the usual troubles. There came a wind, and "I thought by grab we was gonna lose 'em all." But "We rounded up the herd and put 'em on the cars, and that was the last of the old Two Bars."

But not quite. "When I got to the boss and tried to draw my roll. He had me figgered out nine dollars in the hole." So the lonesome cowboy, presumably singing the gladsome refrain, "coma ti yi, yippy, yippy-a, yippy-a," concludes philsophically:

"I'll sell my outfit as soon as I can. And I wouldn't punch cows for no danged man."

We used to know a few verses of that old song ourself, but we doubt if any of the ones we knew were ever published in cold type. However, we wouldn't be surprised to see them spelled out cold-turkey in some modern novel, if we read modern novels.

The last train drive from Texas to Montana and Wyoming was made around 1893, but while it lasted—close to thirty years—it was one of the most extraordinary phenomenons in American economic history. Its like will never be seen again on this earth, though we understand some parts of Australia still indulge the practice.

THE WRAPPING OF GIFTS

December 22, 1953

We wish to pay deserved tribute at this time to the people, mostly women, who devote their time and talents to gift-wrapping merchandise as Christmas presents. And the art takes plenty of talent and time.

We pay this tribute with heartfelt sympathy, for hardly a Christmas passes but we find ourself jammed into a corner somewhere with a peck of trouble on our hands. It always seems to work out so we have to wrap and prepare for mailing at least one Christmas present, or several going to the same address, and we always emerge from this encounter fit to be tied, ourself, and delivered to the nearest psychiatrist.

At all other times there is enough wrapping paper, fancy and plain, around the house to fill every garbage can on our alley; but as sure as our annual agony approaches, it's all gone. String is another commodity encountered in great plenty—until you need some to tie up a Christmas package.

After acquiring paper and twine, at considerable time and trouble, you square off against your task. That is when your real trouble begins. Apt as not, you leave something out and have to open up again to rectify the oversight. Try as you may, you can't make a good smooth job of the wrapping. Instead of the neatness and trimness the professionals achieve, the bundle that finally leaves your hands looks like something right fresh off the city dump.

But somehow you manage to get the thing fixed up ready for the label or tag that is to direct it to the recipient. These are never available when needed. You are

either fresh out of labels and tags, or they have been put away somewhere beyond recollection or reach.

And if you're lucky to locate one finally, you can find there isn't a drop of ink in the house, fountain pen or otherwise.

Yes, we admire the gift and package wrappers; what a neat and finished job they turn out! As for us, we'd rather dig a ditch or grub mesquite trees off a half-acre of ground. Not near as frustrating.

CHRISTMAS NEUROSES

December 22, 1954

Now comes a psychiatrist who says many people suffer a "Christmas neurosis," not because they lost a loved one on that date or because of a Scrooge temperament, but that they were disappointed in childhood when they fancied brother or sister got a better present

than they did. Their conscious mind might long ago have forgotten the slight, but their subconscious turns them against Christmas—hence the "Christmas neurosis."

We suppose we were born lucky, next to the last of a family of a round dozen boys and girls. The division of Christmas presents at our house was even-handed. Into each stocking went an apple, an orange, a few gumdrops and other assorted candies. For the girls there were extras in the form of ribbons for the hair, or perhaps a sachet, and for each boy a small bunch of Chinese firecrackers and on especially prosperous occasions a roman candle or two.

That was all. No complaints, at least no audible complaints. It was generally understood among us that while he might wear a full set of whiskers as Santa Claus, the dispenser of our trinkets wore a wire-tough mustache in real life and would brook no nonsense.

In common with most of our contemporaries, any little extra we got for Christmas was the product of toil, like picking cotton or seeing after the neighbors' livestock.

And while we may have picked up a few little neuroses here and there, like being afraid of a man with a razor strop in his hand, or a lady with a peachtree switch, we managed to escape any Christmas neurosis, and somehow reached adulthood still believing in Santa Claus, as a principle.

THE WINTER SOLSTICE

December 22, 1954

As our local Weather Bureau reminds us, we are now in the shortest days of the year in these latitudes. Starting December 18 and running through the 22d, there were only 601 minutes of daylight as against 849 minutes of darkness. Starting Thursday, the 23d, there will be 602 minutes of daylight and 848 minutes of darkness. This progressive change will continue until next June.

It's the winter solstice.

Meantime, for those who rise early, the morning skies have presented a beautiful Christmasy effect. Venus, the brightest of the planets, has been the morning star, and not far off the last quarter of the moon has draped its crescent effect in the morning sky. Some other star or planet has been in close proximity to Venus, heightening the effect of that planet's natural brightness. With a bit of imagination one would well believe the scene might be a duplicate of that some 1,954 years ago.

THE GUARDIAN ANGEL

December 24, 1954

The British Medical Journal has come through with a reassuring word to parents about Santa Claus. There is no harm in telling children that there is a Santa Claus, says this official publication of the British Medical Association.

Young children, it says, "tend not to differentiate between reality and make-believe, and will be content to live with heroes who are partly fact and partly fiction."

If children take gory nursery rhymes in their stride without permanent harmful effects—and some of them are real scary—why quibble over the merry old gentleman who passes as Santa Claus?

Surely no nobler hero was ever invented. He is the symbol of all that is kind and gentle and beautiful, the perfect antidote for all the cold realities of life that children must gradually get used to.

Even grownups have a hard enough time staying on an even keel in a world filled with violence, with betrayals, with backbiting and backstabbing. We all have to believe in a Santa Claus-type hero to a certain extent to retain our sanity. A life of unrelieved worry, regret and disappointment would make neurotics of us all.

So we fix our faith on the infinite mercies of God, and we believe in the unseen things of heaven and earth that make life endurable under the most adverse circumstances. And if we are wise we do not scoff at the faith of a little child, and we do not carry around a bottle of testing-acid to apply to things of which we cannot always be sure—such as love, friendship and trust in one another.

Of course, as Virginia O'Hanlon was assured by the New York Sun 50-odd years ago, there is a Santa Claus. There just simply has to be a Santa Claus, just as there has to be a guardian angel for each and everyone.

Merry Christmas, All

December 24, 1954

The huge fellow in a red white-trimmed suit, his whiskers flowing, called us over to his booth and introduced himself as Santa Claus. Wanted to know what we'd like for Christmas, then cannily untracked himself by asking if we'd been a good little boy. In the interest of truth and the Christmas spirit, we said yes, we'd been a good little boy—some 50-odd years ago.

We had too, aside from a few little faults too trivial to mention, like failing to keep our black ribbed stockings pulled up over our long itchy underwear, letting our shirttail hang out, and washing behind the ears only when stood over by a parent breathing dire threats.

We had always been prompt to bring in the firewood when asked, providing the request was accompanied by an admonition that if we didn't attend to that chore immediately we'd have to go without supper. Even so, there was a verbal hedge if the weather was cold: "Wellum, wait'll I warm."

We told a reasonable facsimile of the truth when hemmed in an inescapable corner. "Did you tie a can to

Mr. Smith's dog's tail?" No, we never tied no can to no dog's tail, and that was the literal truth. We had merely provided the can and the string, and held the dog while somebody else did the tying.

Had we taken our capsule of anti-chill medicine? Yessum, of course we had. That also was the literal truth; we had taken it out to the back porch and thrown it in the weeds.

Most of us were good little boys and girls while of Santa Claus age, at least for a few days before the great event.

Why does Santa Claus always ask children if they've been good? A leading question, verily, and if the answer is evasive Santa Claus has only himself to blame. And isn't it sort of sinful to place children in that kind of predicament—having to tell a fib to escape punishment and receive a reward for exemplary conduct?

Merry Christmas. Thanks for all the cards and the presents and the kind words. And from all of us here at the Reporter-News to all of you 47,000 subscribing families in this area, a Happy and prosperous New Year.

CHRISTMAS AT COPPERAS COVE

December 18, 1955

We don't know if this is a proper Christmas story
or not, but we have been wanting to tell it for a long
time and if it isn't exactly factual it isn't fictional either,
but a compound of both, for what is truth except the
essence that is distilled out of a man's memory of things
experienced, things seen and felt, things heard, things
dreamed of and wished for—even things feared and
derided. Some people say Santa Claus is an arrant old
fraud himself, but we know better than that. So you'll
have to make up your own mind whether it's truth or
fiction for after almost fifty years we are a bit confused
about some of the details ourself.

There came into our little Central Texas community set in a cove of the calcareous hills a man and his wife
and their son Walter. It's odd, but Walter's is the only
name we recall. They were obviously of ancient peasant
stock from somewhere between the Elbe and the Oder.
Poppa looked old and beat-up at 40, bent with toil, his
arms swinging down to his knees—the very caricature of
a man; even his walk was like that of an ape, a sort of

113

swinging lurch, from long stooping in the fields.
Momma still wore the outlandish clothes she landed in,
and continued to do so for years for this was a very poor
family. Walter was a towhead and as quiet and subdued
as his parents.

After a year or two of working for other farmers,
Poppa bought the scrawniest, most run-down farm in
the neighborhood, almost as much rock as soil, and
people criticized the vendor for taking a foreigner
shamelessly in.

But Poppa worked morning, noon and night, moving rocks from the field and building from them fences, a barn, a cowshed, and finally a house half as big as the barn, which seemed to be the custom of his people.

Pretty soon the little farm was yielding a living of sorts and people became accustomed to the odd foreigners when they came to town in the family wagon. Momma would bring in butter and eggs to swap for staples, and Poppa occasionally planked down a few small coins for an axe handle or a pound or two of nails. Walter always tagged along behind his Momma, who always tagged along three paces behind Poppa, for that too was a custom of their country.

The young idlers of the town usually had something cute to say to the trio, though of course they did not understand the language. It was the smart thing to do to say something nasty in a pleasant tone of voice, for the strangers would smile and nod as though they had been complimented. Only one boy refrained from this form of ridicule—Joey, the charcoal burner's son, who spent most of his night hunting coons and possums in the coves and on the ridges with his dog Samson. Joey would walk away in disgust when the raillery started. Once he had been the object of this sort of ribbing, but only once; he had gone at the ribber in a fury of flying fists and that was that.

Well, just before one Christmas—it was the time of the panic in '07—the foreigners came to town and Poppa pulled his team into a vacant lot, dropped the outside traces, wrapped the lines around a standard, and they all got down. They strolled up the main business "street," like three waddling ducks—Poppa, Momma and Walter as always, Poppa in front, Momma in the middle, and Walter behind.

Momma went into the general store with her basket of eggs and butter. Poppa went to the hardware emporium, and Walter, eyes a-bug, drank in the few Christmas goods and decorations visible along the street.

Our gang was in rare good form, and started to pester Walter, who said nothing. Joey went off around the corner with a frown of distaste on his face.

Minutes later here came Poppa from the hardware store with a hand held behind his back, and Momma from the grocery with a few skimpy purchases in her apron. They met where Walter was absorbed in a Christmas display.

Poppa tapped Walter on the shoulder and the youngster whirled. Poppa brought his hand out from behind his back and displayed a hugh coconut with the husk still on.

"Look, Valtar!" he cried, his face split in a rare smile. "Coocoonut! Coom, Valtar, we go home. What

you say, Chris'mas now, eh! Coom, Valtar—
Coocoonut!"

Walter danced in glee, his face shining. And so they
set off toward their wagon—Poppa marching proudly
ahead, Momma coming next, and Walter dancing
around them. Momma's care-worn face was wreathed in
a smile that glowed, and there was happiness and pride
in her eyes. It was the first time we learned joy could
transfigure an ugly face into a beautiful one.

We all laughed out loud, of course; it was so funny.
For years "'Com, Valtar, coocoonut'" was good for a

laugh anytime. (How were we to know that industry and frugality and faith could work such miracles? How could we know that in time the little house would grow and become a big one, and that Walter would become a noted surgeon?)

Well, anyway, about that time Joey came around one corner and that tattletale, pigtailed brat of a sister of his came around the other corner, and the little stinker screamed: "Joey's got a coconut and he won't give me any! The old stingygut!"

Joey was furious. "Shut your mouth, you little fool! I ain't got no coconut neither! You mind your own business."

Well, we got a good laugh out of that too, but not out loud, knowing Joey. And it took this writer about six months to figure out what Joey had done with his coconut, since we always were a little slow on the uptake.

We hear Joey never did turn out very well, but there is a tender spot in our heart for him all the same. We can't imagine what he used for money in acquiring his own little private gift of the Magi, but we can imagine St. Dismas, the penitent Thief, sort of rides herd on Joey's kind. Anyhow, Joey is one of our boyhood heroes, for it was he who taught us a valuable lesson, and a great truth that Santa Claus doesn't necessarily wear a red suit, talk in a bluff, hearty voice and sport a full set of whiskers. He can also play the role of a ragged, dirty little boy right up to the hilt.

BY THE FLICKERING FIRE

December 19, 1955

Most of our older citizens agree that a fireplace is a wasteful, inefficient, messy and generally unsatisfactory way to heat a home. Nevertheless, with the approach of Christmas their thoughts begin to dwell on the time when "hearth and home" meant literally quite a lot more to our way of life than it does now.

In the old days the hearth was the heart of the home. That is where the family gathered for comfort, for good fellowship, for renewal of faith and hope, and for the enjoyment of life. It is pretty difficult to draw these virtues from a hole in the floor or wall out of which heated air emerges. We doubt if anybody ever got inspiration from a radiator or a floor furnace.

Nevertheless between the comfort of a well-heated home and the old style fireplace there is no comparison. That magic little doodad, the thermostat, does all the work that is necessary. No ashes to be removed. No wood to be chopped and brought in. No cold draft down the back of your neck when someone opens the front door. No freezing on one side and blistering on the other.

And yet something is lacking. The symbolism of the fireside isn't there. That one spot in the oldtime home that meant fellowship and family solidarity to young and old alike is missing. You can't stare into a wall heater and daydream of bountiful things as you could with a fireplace. A hot-air system doesn't paint flickering images on wall and ceiling, as the old fireplace did—images of old friends, of relatives momentarily absent, of scenes and gatherings long cherished.

We feel downright sorry for the rising generation who never had a fireplace to gaze into and to moon over. Oh, sure many modern homes contain fireplaces as a gesture, as a concession to the utilitarian past, but few of them ever know the pungency of a good wood fire, or the glow of coals or the firelight flickering on wall and ceiling.

Something went out of Christmas, and out of family life, when the hearth and all it stood for was pushed aside by the gadget age.

THE WONDERFUL PEOPLE

December 27, 1955

Our story, "Christmas at Copperas Cove," which appeared as an editorial in the edition of Sunday, December 18, seems to have attracted considerable attention, and we are deeply appreciative.

The several points it sought to bring out seem to have registered on our readers, and nothing is more flattering and gratifying to a writer than to be understood.

As the story said, it was neither fact nor fiction, but a combination of both. The "coocoonut" incident was entirely true, and remains vivid in our recollection after 48 years; that is, we did witness the transfer of the gift from father to son, and the magical transformation it wrought on father, son and mother.

The rest, alas, was largely poetic license. We say this because a gracious lady wrote from a West Texas community to tell us that she and her father, long-ago residents of Copperas Cove, instantly recognized "Walter" and "Joey."

Well, that's a horse on us; for all we knew about Walter was his given name; and we have known a dozen or more assorted Joeys who could fit into that role. Joey was a prototype of all the hundreds of individuals young and old we have known who go about doing good, and hiding their charities and kindnesses under a bushel basket. There are many of them—rich man, poor man, beggar man, thief.

We would like to acknowledge our lady correspondent's kindly note, but unfortunately we could not quite decipher her surname. This convinces us she did indeed attend the same high school we did. At that she writes a far better hand than we ever could.

Incidently, we wrote the story in less than 45 minutes, while immured at home with a cold, a few days before publication date. Correction: the story wrote itself.

Anyway, we are grateful for the expressions of approval it brought, which is confirmation of the story's central theme: namely, that there are a lot of wonderful people in the world.

Swapper's Paradise

December 27, 1955

We suppose there will be the usual number of returns and exchanges of Christmas gifts this week, always a problem for some stores.

In this connection a little story out of Little Rock last Friday seems apropos. A Christmas tree salesman said a woman brought back a tree she had bought and wanted to exchange it because it somehow didn't seem to fit into her living room.

The salesman told her to take her choice, so she toured the miniature forest of small trees while the salesman returned the rejected specimen to its proper place. Finally the uncertain lady made up her mind—and picked the identical tree she had just returned as unsatisfactory.

A lot of people, male and female, are troubled with the problem of deciding just exactly what they want. They spend many minutes, taking up a salesman's time, deciding between two items turned out by the same manufacturer and as exactly alike as production skill can make them.

That, of course, is part of the fun of shopping.

Like the lady and the Christmas tree, quite often they become dissatisfied with the purchase and come back to make a second choice. And like that lady, they couldn't tell the difference between the two items if they were going to be hanged.

So, if you're unimpressed by that necktie someone sent you for Christmas, just put it away and pass it along to someone else next year. There is a good chance by then that you'll take a liking to it and decide to keep it after all.

Happy hunting, you exchange fans.

LETTERS TO SANTA

December 13, 1956

The New York Postoffice has received so far 6,300 letters to Santa Claus, and no doubt other postoffices throughout the country have received their share. Sample: "My mother hollers at me for drinking all the milk. Please send me a cow."

For many years, until sometime in the 'thirties, this newspaper printed letters to Santa Claus, complete with names and addresses. It fell to us to read and prepare these letters for publication, and one year they numbered more than 1,100. We finally had to discontinue this practice for two reasons: the volume became so great that it was physically impossible to accommodate them all, and it would not have been cricket to leave any of them out; second, the number of phony letters—written by grown-ups or by adolescents, and signed by some friend's name as a means of kidding him—grew to such proportions that some of them began to get into print in spite of all we could do to detect them.

We got to be pretty good at detecting the phonies—most of them were obvious; in some cases we knew the name they bore belonged to grown-ups or adolescents, or the phraseology or the type of request was a dead giveaway—but some of them were so cleverly disguised that they escaped our eagle eye and got into the paper.

We could understand why an adolescent would want to play a trick on a friend, or more often an enemy, but we never could figure out why a grownup would butt into what was intended for tiny tots only.

Well, anyway, for these and other reasons we had to abandon our annual Christmas section devoted to letters to Santa Claus—they sometimes ran on for page after page—and while we were glad to shed an onerous chore, we always got a real thrill out of the real letters, and missed them terribly for the first few years.

What could be more genuine and completely disarming than a real letter from a real child to a Santa Claus who is real to the child?

Incidentally we would examine that request for a cow with microscopic care. A little too adult to be genuine.

SELECTIVE SELECTIONS

December 17, 1956

We have been doing our elite Christmas shopping in the pages of that sterling magazine, the New Yorker, and are glad to report we have completed the chore with complete satisfaction to our own sense of taste and what we hope will be the joy of our friends, relatives and in-laws.

For a bookish friend we picked up a paper-bound volume of a paper written by a Frenchman on the Yellow Fever Epidemic in Philadelphia in 1793, a steal for $45. Even that far back there were those who contended that yellow fever was contagious, but it took a Walter Reed to prove it.

We selected a camel's-hair polo coat for ourself at $135, and for a friend a set of silver chessmen in a leather case for $1,900. For a dear old lady of our acquaintance who once said our work reminded her of Henry W. Grady we acquired a car robe for $195.

There is an interesting story about that polo coat mentioned above, incidentally. We deliberately rejected one for $350 which the seller claimed required the pelts of 43 Kashmir Mountain goats, none of which ever grazed at lower altitude than 23,000 feet. Think of depriving goats of their warm clothing at such frigid altitudes!

For a cowpunch friend of long standing we fell with cries of joy on a pair of chaps for $250, and to top it off and make his Christmas complete we picked up a belt and pistol holster at a trifling $400.

We were unfortunately unable to make up our mind in a fine display of watches selling for $39.50 up to $10,000. They stocked not a one for $7,500, which we

had made up our mind not to pay more than. The little woman will have to wait.

We are grateful to the magazine for all this Christmas cheer, which was ours for a pittance—only 20 cents per copy.

THE SCENTS OF CHRISTMAS

December 18, 1957

To the small child of fifty and sixty years ago
Christmas meant many things.

It meant unfamiliar but pleasant smells, such as that
given off by apples and oranges, where apples and oranges were not among the staples of family diet. It
meant the tantalizing smell of pies baking and turkey
roasting. It meant the tang of peppermint candy, in long
red-striped sticks, a dozen sticks to the bundle.

It meant the scent of mothballs, not disagreeable at
all, but exotic and exciting, especially to the small boy
who had picked cotton at 25 cents a hundredweight and
bought himself a pair of high buttoned shoes and a cap
to go with the suit of clothes Dad had bought as his
Christmas surprise. The scent of mothballs was in the
clothes, for in those days new clothes fresh from the
store always reeked with this odor. Therefore mothballs
were definitely a part of Christmas and all the pleasant
things that can happen to a small boy at Christmastime.

The scent of burning cornstalks still hung in the air
as late as Christmas, and nothing could linger longer in

memory. It symbolized the end of harvest, and spoke of long weekends tramping the fields and the woods to worry the skittish cottontail, or trap the fat succulent quail, or contest with the possum for the purple persimmon and its velvet-smooth fruit.

The little girls, scrubbed to a shine, their pigtails in colored ribbons, and their clothes starched like parchment, smelled sweetest of all to the small boy who accidentally brushed against one of them as they lined up for the Christmas program.

"Backward, turn backward O Time, in thy flight; make me a child again, just for tonight!"

PRESENTS FOR DAD

December 4, 1958

What to get father for Christmas never was much of a problem in most families. Then as now the principal problem was to get him a generous mood.

But the character of Christmas presents for father has undergone great changes in the last several decades.

Practical gifts were the order of the old days. A mustache cup was a standby. A gold-leafed shaving mug for his rack in the barber shop. A humidor for his favorite pipe tobacco, or—if the family was in funds—a meerschaum or calabash pipe.

A necktie of course. If Junior was doing the buying, it was apt to be a necktie so loud Dad wouldn't wear it, but Junior would. (And if you think Junior didn't take that into account, you didn't know the adolescent male of fifty years ago very well.)

Socks, of course—good heavy woollen ones. A good woollen muffler, too. Teen-age concern for Dad's health and comfort was a touching thing: though Dad might be no more than crowding forty, the offspring persisted in regarding him as ancient of days, tottering on the brink of senility.

133

Socks, neckties and handkerchiefs are still the most popular as Christmas gifts—in the eyes of the givers, at least, or so it seems to Dad.

One Christmas the kids ganged up, pooled their resources, and gave Dad a rosewood whatnot—just what mother needed for the parlor.

Larry Chittenden a Real Personage

December 11, 1958

Larry Chittenden has been dead these 24 years (September, 1934) but the Cowboy Christmas Ball he inspired is making its usual pre-Christmas run at Anson, with the final round scheduled for tonight.

The original Christmas ball Larry Chittenden made famous took place at the Star Hotel in Anson in 1885. It was revived in 1934, the year of his death, and has been going like a house afire every year since. It comes as near being as unique a holiday event as Texas affords, and the people of Anson are due a great deal of credit for making it an outstanding occasion, carried on as near to its orginal pattern as possible.

The ballad which it commemorates was a rollicking one, full of local color and with the real names of the original participants woven in.

It so happens this writer knew Larry (William Lawrence) Chittenden quite well, from about 1915 until he died. We interviewed him on numerous occasions, and corresponded with him betweenwhiles. He was born in Montclair, N.J., March 23, 1862, and worked as a

135

newspaper reporter in New York City. In 1883 he came
to Texas as a traveling salesman and correspondent, on a
borrowed capital of $50. He started a ranch near Anson
with his uncle, a Brooklyn congressman, in 1887, and
soon after bought his uncle out.

He finally put together a spread of 10,000 acres, but
spent most of his time in his latter years at various
homes—one in Red Bank, N.J., a winter home in Palm
Beach, and a summer home at Christmas Cove, Me.,
where he founded a unique autograph free library. His
visits back to his Texas properties became more infre-

quent in his later years (he died at 72), but he always seemed to enjoy them, and his love of West Texas people never waned. The lad from New Jersey was completely fascinated with the speech, customs and pastimes of cowboys, as his Christmas ballad showed.

He became widely know as the "the poet ranchman." His Ranch Verses, brought out in 1893, had gone through 16 printings by 1929 and his Bermuda Verses (1909) contained some of his finest work. A critic called his "Wild White Steeds of Neptune" on a par with the best of Tennyson. (Larry Chittenden loved the sea and the ranch country in about equal proportions.)

He was a dapper little man, as neat as a pin, his mustache always in perfect trim, his manners impeccable, his voice gentle and low. His last letter to us, shortly before he died, asked for imformation on oil prospects in Reeves County, where it seemed he owned a couple of sections.

It was a privilege to have known Larry Chittenden, "the poet ranchman," and a great gentleman.

CHRISTMAS SHOPS ARE ALL A-GLOW

December 8, 1959

Christmas shopping is off with a whoop and a holler, and before the dust settles on Christmas Eve a few of the standing records may well be smashed—at least in our town and territory.

The goods are plentiful, beautifully displayed, and tempting beyond measure.

How Christmas has changed in this century!

In the old days it was largely a matter of hanging up your stocking to the mantel, snuggling down under the covers, and keeping one weather eye open to spy on Santa Claus while he filled them with peppermint stick candy, a-napple and a-norange, a batch of firecrackers and, for the older boys, a skyrocket or two and some Roman candles.

That was it. When times were good—say, when cotton was above six cents a pound—a family might blow in as much as five or six dollars on Christmas surprises, but seldom more, for that was all they could afford.

Now the sky's the limit—or one's credit is the limit.

Children's toys were strictly for Christmas in those days, and the kids managed somehow to make them last for months and to wring the last mite of pleasure and enjoyment out of them.

Now toys and "playthings" are year-round things: every time a kid turns around somebody shoves a new one in his hands, and the custom has become so commonplace that children miss the surprise and pleasure of getting them for Christmas.

As a male Christmas shopper we are probably the world's worst; indeed, we imagine most men find it irksome and a pain in the neck, but with women it's different; they are natural-born shoppers.

Like many men, we long ago took the coward's way out—we turned the Christmas shopping chore over to our lady.

No longer do we invade the lingerie department, slink furtively up to the counters and display cases of unmentionables, and stammer our way through the selection of something suitable for a lady.

We quit when we had trouble finding a fascinator. The trouble we had was in making modern salesladies understand what a fascinator was. They'd never heard of such a thing.

140

MERRY CHRISTMAS

December 24, 1959

The only full holiday of the year observed by this newspaper is Christmas Day. By long standing custom we do not issue a paper December 25, but the full publishing schedule will be resumed with Saturday morning and Sunday morning's editions.

This gives the night crew Christmas Eve off, and the day crew Christmas Day off. We feel sure our subscribers don't begrudge them this one day of the year to enjoy the occasion with family, relatives and friends.

The editor at this juncture would like to express his thanks for the many Christmas and New Year letters and cards that have come his way, in lieu of more intimate and personal thanks.

They are deeply appreciated. It is a grand feeling to be thought of at Christmastime above all others when of all times the spirit of good will and good cheer is abroad in the land, and in all hearts.

Christmas doesn't belong exclusively to children, though quite properly it is a child's holiday above all others—a holiday dedicated to the Child in the Manger.

There is a bit of the child in most of us from the greatest to the humblest. Indeed, "great" and "humble" are almost synonymous terms for where there is greatness there is also humility.

The true spirit of Christmas is indestructible for it abides in the hearts of all civilized mankind now and forever more.

The giving and receiving of gifts, the carols and the countless manifestations of joy and gladness, the tinsel and the glitter—all these and more are but the outward show of what we call Christmas, the window-dressing so to speak.

The real spirit of Christmas lies deep in the human heart often inexpressible, sometimes obscured by trivialities, but always present where good will and love of humanity prevails—which in spite of a great deal of noisy evidence to the contrary, is a much more universal human trait than the cynic imagines.

Merry Christmas!

MARVELOUS WORLD OF LITTLE CHILDREN

December 24, 1959

What was the happiest Christmas you can recall?

Think hard, now. Wasn't it almost the first one you can remember, when you were a child filled with wonders of the world?

There were stockings attached to the mantel, the night before. Into each stocking with even-handed impartiality, Santa Claus had placed a handful of English walnuts, six sticks of red peppermint candy, an apple and an orange, some flat discs of sweet-scented candy with sentimental messages imprinted on them, a package of small Chinese firecrackers, some sparklers, and if the price of cotton had been good, a small mechanical toy of some sort, perhaps a tin mouse that scooted across the bare floor when you wound its rubber band, scaring the girls to pieces, the silly things.

For the larger boys large enough to be trusted with such dangerous things, there would be some Roman candles and skyrockets—skyrockets that performed spectacularly long before the late Dr. Goddard started to experiment with his rockets on the sands of New

143

Mexico. What started as a toy has become today the Number 1 threat to human existence on this earth.

Fireworks are out, legally, in this and many another town, and a good thing, but in the old days firecrackers, Roman candles—or cannon, we never knew the correct term—and skyrockets were staples of the Old Christmastide. (Note: The dictionary says it's Roman candles, but in our boyhood everybody said "cannons".)

So, the happiest Christmas was in your childhood. There was just the right mixture of wonder and belief, a wonder never again to be recreated in its pristine purity, and a belief that defied all the arts of sophistication and cynicism to weaken in the slightest degree.

It was a good world, a world filled with delight and sheer enjoyment, a world in which Pa and Ma, Grandpa and Grandma were just about the greatest people inhabiting the earth, and even one's brothers and sisters were fit to associate with at times.

A lost world, perhaps, but lost only to grownups. To children, God love and bless them, it remains a beautiful and marvelous world, a world in which a little boy named Jesus was King in Bethlehem.

Thank You, May the Lord Bless You

December 23, 1960

Soon, as a sort of grand windup of Christmas, the loudspeakers, newspaper classified columns, billboards and other means of spreading the glad tidings of appreciation will blossom with warm, sympathetic and appreciative words of kindness.

If this is phrased in time-worn and partly lurid words, forget it; no offense is meant, and certainly that particular style has been in use for generations.

For weeks we had the feeling that our readers, including more than 55,000 paid-up subscribers, could get along very well without hearing from us this New Year's, to say nothing of Christmas.

Then habit got the better of us, and we reached for our typewriter. One isn't likely to grind out 500,000 words of editorial matter a year for more than forty years without having it shape into a sort of habit on him.

Then we thought of all those children whose fathers and mothers were born and brought up in Abilene—three generations or more—under our gabby regime.

And our course was clear. There was our subject, at least an excuse for a writing orgy. Hurray!

At our elbow is a Christmas card from Mrs. Harry Oder's first grade class at Austin School in Abilene. There are many familiar names there, though we never saw them to know who's who; we know their parents and grandparents—bless them all.

This is one letter among hundreds. Abilene's six Junior and Senior High schools and whole schools and classes among the grades wrote hundreds and hundreds of letters to this editor in the last few months. It never

happened to any individual before, least of all to us.

As far as we can tell, this was a miracle. We are not conscious in any sense of deserving such attention. We can't recall having performed any civic duty entitling us to such attention.

But we are grateful, though feeling unworthy.

We have tried to be loyal to our job, our employers, our co-workers, our fellow Abilenians. We still belong to the same church congregation we joined when we came to Abilene Dec. 4, 1914. Our father, grandfather and great grandfather and numerous uncles, inlaws and whatnots, were Methodist preachers all the way back to John and Charles Wesley's time. So our church is St. Paul's, though we are ashamed we haven't served it better. We never belonged to any fraternal organization; just weren't a "joiner."

We thought a great deal about this article before finally deciding. We decided and undecided not to undertake its writing right up to the last minute. We still don't know that it should, but we feel a compulsion to say "thank you and God bless you" to all those wonderful grownups and children who so signally honored us.

Whatever we are we owe to our association with a grand bunch of people down through the years. We can't recall a living soul we ever worked with that we can't shake hands with and call friend today. Being at "outs" with anybody makes us physically sick.

We could go on this way for a long time, but won't. God bless everybody!—(F.G.)